Knight Book of Howlers

A surefooted animal is an animal that
when it kicks it does not miss.

Please sir,
Billy's ill with swellings in his throat and
the doctor says it's a gathering of the
clans.

Debate: Something used in fishing, I put
debate on the hook.

Gladiator: What the cannibal said.

A prospectus is a man who looks for gold.

Knight Book of Howlers

Collected and illustrated by
Richard E. Gregory

KNIGHT BOOKS
Hodder & Stoughton

ISBN 0 340 20 227 0
Copyright © 1977 Richard E. Gregory
First published in 1977

Printed and bound in Great Britain in Knight Books for
Hodder & Stoughton Children's Books, a division of Hodder &
Stoughton Ltd, Arlen House, Salisbury Road, Leicester by
Richard Clay (The Chaucer Press) Ltd, Bungay, Suffolk

Contents

Acknowledgement

I acknowledge my indebtedness for this collection to those teachers who passed on howlers garnered from their own classes; to colleagues who retailed others from memory; to the unknown who left a number in a tattered exercise book I found in a classroom cupboard; but most of all to the many hundreds of children, black and white, who in innocence succeeded in raising a smile when a smile was most needed.

And underneath there hangs the milk.

Introduction

The trouble with howlers is that the layman finds it hard to believe they are genuine. He seems to have a sneaking suspicion that they are manufactured by a team of retired schoolteachers working behind closed doors in some remote room at one of the smaller Universities.

But he is wrong.

True howlers are never manufactured intentionally. They just happen. A connoisseur has little trouble spotting the fakes.

The drudgery of examinations and the tedious business of marking hundreds of papers is not sufficient to quench the flame of hope flickering in the bosom of the average teacher. He knows that sooner or later, his probing red pen will uncover another gem. Then the busy silence of the staff room will be disturbed by sedate titters, or vulgar laughter, as he shares the find with his colleagues.

Unhappily, each profession has its quota of unethical members and the scholastic profession is no exception. It must be accepted therefore, that there is a low type of teacher who spends part of his spare time inventing howlers. Luckily, most of these are easily detected by the expert and rejected. But a few get by and where they could have been conceived on a basis of truth and are sufficiently funny, they have been preserved.

Such a one is the following classic, an essay on a cow,

which we are asked to believe was written by an African schoolboy, "The cow is a mammal and also a domestic animal. She is covered with ox hide. At the back is a tail with a puff for to chase away the flies because they make all kinds of sick. The head is in front where grow the horns and the mouth is situated. The horns are to bump and the mouth to bellow. Underneath the cow hangs the milk and it is arranged that when you touch it the milk flows out. The milk never gives in except sometimes. The cow makes milk and how she does it nobody knows. She has a fine sense of smell. You smell it from afar. She makes the whole farm to smell.

The husband of the cow is the ox. He looks just like the cow but there hangs no milk. Therefore he is not a mammal. He is used to work. The young of the cow is the calf. This is not the same as in the leg which is a mussel. That is all I know about the cow."

Another howler which is suspect but which deserves to be remembered, describes the incident when Sir Walter Raleigh placed his cloak over a puddle to enable Queen Elizabeth to cross dry shod, "Her Majesty remarked to Sir Walter, 'I'm afraid I've spoiled your cloak.' To which the gallant knight replied, 'Dieu et mon droit,' which means, 'My God, and you're right!'"

With the exception of these two, the rest of the howlers in this collection are, to the best of my knowledge, reproduced as they first appeared, uncontaminated by the hand of a teacher.

I was prompted to start this anthology when I found a tattered notebook in a cupboard in the classroom of a colleague who handed over everything, 'lock, stock and barrel', before he left the country. Inside, were howlers he had been collecting for several years. I began to add to them.

Teachers and others who have much to do with children will recognise some of them as old friends. This is not surprising, particularly if they are based on spelling errors. Such a one is, "Martin Luther was executed by a bull", which to my knowledge has appeared regularly for the last forty years.

Certain howlers turn up so regularly, a cynic might suspect that teachers with a warped sense of humour are planting the seed from which they grow in the fertile minds of their pupils and waiting mischievously to see it burgeon.

Be that as it may, there are some children bright enough to see possibilities in a carelessly worded question and come up with a howler.

Who can blame the boy, when being asked to put certain words into sentences, found two of them, 'scantily' and 'hastily' in close juxtaposition and wrote, "Some of the girls were scantily clad. The Minister left hastily for home."

But one is left wondering whether it was ignorance or malice that led an African student at the school graduating party to ask for a "caustic soda for the Principal, please", when all the man wanted was a Scotch and soda.

It should not be thought that children and students are the only perpetrators of howlers. The most unlikely people can do it. Sign writers are an example. You would think they would check and double check before offering their work to the public gaze. Nevertheless, they do, on occasion, produce fine examples of their kind.

This gem, at the end of a list of rules posted at a

swimming pool, was enjoyed by thousands over a long, hot summer, "These rules and regulations must be obeyed, or you will be bared."

Even professional writers, who should know better, are sometimes guilty of producing howlers. They are reluctant to admit this and tend to pass the blame on to the printer. But the reporter who was responsible for the following from the *Vancouver Sun* had no such alibi, "Even in later years with his long iron-grey hair standing 6 ft 1 in and weighing about 200 lbs, Duke was an impressive figure in Waikiki."

Diana, aged ten, wrote a review of a book she had been told to read. She summed up, "This is a very good book for those people who like to read a lot before they get to the exciting part."

There are no exciting parts in this book, but I hope the reader will find there is much to make him laugh.

1. Spell it!

Spelling has always been a problem which even modern methods of education have been unable to solve. It is not too difficult to instruct children to write reasonably legibly, but many a teacher has despaired of ever planting correct spelling habits into the English-speaking young.

It was not surprising therefore, when a parent received a report card on his child which read, "The dawn of legibility in his handwriting reveals his almost total inability to spell."

And it was probably this inability to spell that prompted one student to write, "The masculine of belle is stomack."

Children will rarely make spelling mistakes deliberately but they will often write badly to conceal ignorance, although the bolder ones are quite capable of actually admitting to a lack of knowledge rather than submitting a blank paper, presumably on the theory that an examiner prefers something to nothing. Here are some examples.

"There are four symptoms of a cold, two I forget and the other two are well known."

"The names of five animals that live in the Amazon jungles is armerdillos and four others."

"What do you know of Abraham Lincoln? – I

can't answer that as we are not doing Old Testament now."

"How long is Lake Michigan? – Frifly big."

Many howlers happen because the child has been using unfamiliar words. Children like to use new words but they often confuse them with other words of similar sound, or even of the same superficial appearance. So there was some excuse for the boy who wrote, "When a person goes to the tropics, they should get intoxicated first", and his friend who said, "In the United States people are put to death by elocution."

Many children never see the words of the songs they sing, so they simply repeat what they think they hear, often with startling results.

"How can a mother's tender care
  Cease towards a child she bear?"

"Onward Christian soldiers,
  Marching as to war,
  With the Cross of Jesus
  Left behind the door."

"Gentle Jesus meek and mild,
  Look upon a little child.
  Pity mice and pretty me,
  Suffer me to come to Thee."

"Good King Wenceslaus looked stout
  On the feast of Stephen."

"Beneath whose awful hand we hold
  Dominion over rod and line."

A connoisseur is a man who opens taxis
outside a posh hotel.

"Old Susannah don't you cry for me,
  I come from weezy Anna with a Bandaid on my knee."

"We can sing full though we be." (This was how the child
    heard, 'Weak and sinful though we be.')

Sometimes the teacher is at fault. He should never take
for granted that even his simplest statements have been
understood by every individual in his class. If he does, he
can only blame himself when a child writes, as this one
did, "The General had a lovely funeral; it took eight
soldiers to carry the beer", and this, "If anyone faints in
church put her head between the knees of the nearest
doctor."

Nor should he be offended if the members of his class
seek each other's help rather than face ridicule by appeal-
ing to him. The following note passed from one little
girl to another reveals the sort of dilemma that over-
whelms children from time to time.

"How do you spell 'hair' when you mean
'rabbit'?"

But on the other hand, no matter how carefully a
teacher takes a lesson, there is always some member of
the class not paying attention and such a one it must have
been who wrote, "The longest day in the Southern Hemi-
sphere is Sunday."

He probably came from a home where observance of
the Lord's Day meant a strict denial of worldly pleasures.

The child's efforts to express himself sometimes create
a picture which, while vivid, is not necessarily the one he
had in mind, as for example, "Algebraic symbols are

To excavate means to hollow out,
e.g., our baby excavates a lot.

used when you don't know what you are talking about", or, "William ordered his archers to shoot at the thickest part of the English, so they shot upwards so that the arrows would fall on the Englishmen's heads."

Some children are more mentally alert than their answers would at first suggest. Consider, for instance, the following.

"*Q.* What is the half of five?
A. It depends whether you mean two or three."

"To remove air from a flask, fill it with water, tip the water out and put the cork in quick."

"Quadrupeds has no singular. You can't have a horse with one leg."

And the rather timid little girl who wrote, "I used to be frightened of Science but it's all right if you keep your head", had acquired a philosophy many of her elders could emulate with profit.

Other children are sufficiently self-confident to be able to express their thoughts forcefully without having to worry about spelling or syntax, as the following demonstrate.

"The school dinners is very nice but milk pudding is a food I will not eat espeshally tabby oaker."

"Taxes is what people wont pay. They use them to keep the roads nice."

"False witness is when nobody does nothing and somebody goes and tells."

The best thing for a drowned person is to tie their tongue under their chin and make them walk about.

2. Ask a silly question. . .

Children are observant and shrewd. They are also uncomplicated and direct and, in consequence, they watch with suspicion any teacher whose manner is ambiguous. They like to be asked direct questions and are suspicious of anything that smells of trickery or is loaded with innuendo. They hate sarcasm and they get bored with the funny teacher, but at least they know where they stand when they are faced with these classroom trials and react accordingly.

An Inspector paid a visit to a backward class in a tough school.

'Give me a number,' he asked them. There was a glum silence, then somebody growled, 'Twelve.'

The Inspector wrote 21 on the chalkboard, Nobody spoke.

'Not very bright, are they?' he whispered, loudly enough to be heard. 'I'll try them again. All right, give me another.' Again there was silence; then a bored voice said, 'Twenty-three.'

The Inspector wrote 32 on the board. There was a soggy silence. 'I'll try them once more,' he muttered to the teacher. 'Give me another number. Come on now, anybody.' They looked at him blankly, then a voice from the back row said, 'OK. Thirty-three, and let's see you mess about with that.'

It is easy to feel sorry for children pestered by foolish

Felo de se.
Fell in the sea.

questions and difficult to understand why so many of them are ever asked. Why, for instance should a teacher bother to enquire, "Who came first out of the Ark?"

Whatever her reason, she got the delightful answer, "I don't know who came first, but Noah came fourth."

Sometimes questions are set so carelessly that children are led to believe there is some connection between them when in fact they are meant to extract separate answers.

It is easy to see how such a misunderstanding could arise when a child was presented with a paper on which the following appeared:

"Correct these sentences:
    (a) A hen has three legs.
    (b) Who done it?"

His answer, while not exactly the one the teacher was looking for, deserved credit, "The hen never done it, God done it."

Sometimes questions are asked with the best will in the world only to receive, not the reply courteous, but the retort blunt. A little boy fell and hurt himself and his teacher asked, gently consoling, 'Poor darling, did you cry?' To which he replied, 'What was the good, you weren't here.'

In the same category must be placed the remarks of a boy who was explaining the symbols on his report card, "A means excellent. B means good. C means fair. And D is what I got."

The manner in which a question is asked, the personality of the questioner, a weakness in the ability to spell or to hear, or simply a misunderstanding of the problem, all determine the kind of answer the child will produce.

The people of Vennas used to call their king
a dog but they did not prernounce it the same.

But there is another factor, often overlooked, that sometimes influences his response to a question and that is,
environment.

One day, some eager student writing a thesis for a
Ph.D. will perhaps find a social significance in the type of
howler produced by children from schools on either side
of the tracks. He would have no difficulty in assessing the
level of society from which the perpetrator of the following came, "The Soviet is what the middle classes call
their table napkin."

Nor would he hesitate to classify as *très snob*, the
young lady who wrote, "A street is a road with a very
good class of person living in it."

And just as easily, put in his proper place, the boy who
said, "If you are drinking anything, you should not put it
in your saucer but drink it by the handle."

In case anyone should think there is an ultimate level
on the social scale above which the children of the
privileged exist in such a rarefied atmosphere they are
incapable of making the errors of lesser fry, Dermot
Morrah tells a story in his book about the heir to the
throne.

"When Prince Charles was a small boy, a visiting
clergyman talked to the boys at his school about the
Church, comparing it to a ship and preparing to make the
point that Jesus was the Master. 'And who,' he asked, 'is
the most important member of the crew?' And to help
them, he added, 'It begins with a C.' Several hands were
raised. The clergyman pointed to a small, plump boy,
'Please sir,' said Prince Charles, 'the Cook.' "

Ordinary sailors are called aimiable seamen.

3. Candid comments

Children who had been moved from antiquated, over-crowded buildings to a new school were asked to write about what they thought of their new school.

"When the sun shines, it comes in," was the comment of one child.

Some, however, found the size of the new school initially frightening, particularly the more backward, and one little girl wrote, "When I thought I was going to the big, new school, I was frightened. I stepped calmly on the bus trembling all over."

It is good to know she soon found some old friends in "the nice new lavertry".

It was noteworthy that although the children were asked to write only about the buildings, they were reluctant to leave out the staff. On the whole, remarkable tact was shown, even in expressing dislike.

"Even the nasty teachers are nice, really."
"I expect it is us who are wrong."

One realist wrote, "I think the teachers have a great responsible with the children", while a juvenile cynic observed, "There are eight people on the teaching staff and three people on the working staff."

But the nail was hit on the head by the child who wrote, "I like this school because of my teacher, really."

There is no doubt that for good or ill, the teacher is

Widows should be cleaned sometimes.

the hub of the child's school universe and we must balance, "I like it because we have a good staff and they help you in trouble", with what lies behind, "Here you get a new start and it gives you training to be polite."

The teachers do mean a great deal to the children, but bulking next in strength of comment came the delight in what are perhaps best called extended interests.

The physical education facilities were rapturously commented on by those who on wet days were deprived of PE or who attempted an attenuated form of it while imprisoned by desks.

Here is an example, "... a gymnasium as well, with climbing stands and ropes hanging from beams to swarm up. One never knows when these arts will be useful."

A subject called Science, but frequently misspelt, is welcomed, "There are a lot of wonderful things here, including central heating, games day and queer chemistry."

Sanitation was touched on by more than one who had unhappy memories of the old school, "The new school is kept clean and tidy to keep up with the newness of the buildings", and "In the new school we don't need to keep all our clothes on in the winter."

But there was also the not to be stilled, small voice from one of the old schools, "We all hope the new school will be respectable when finished."

Following a lecture on Road Safety which included instruction on the care of bicycles, children were asked to write an essay on the subject. One nine-year-old came up with, "It is no use having a nice clean bicycle if the nuts come off", which was only one step removed from the warning uttered by his friend a year younger, "You mustn't ride a bike if the chain is off."

Chivalry is when you feel cold.

Still mechanically alert, although with his thoughts on the beckoning pool, another child in the same grade wrote, "If you go swimming you must see that the steering is straight."

Another youngster, suffering apparently from a slight feeling of disappointment, reported on an accident he had seen, "But nobody was killed, just a bit hurt."

He described how he went to tell a policeman, " 'Good morning,' I said. And so did he."

And later in his account he wrote, "Friday nights and Saturday mornings are the best times for accidents."

Perhaps this was because, "Only on certain nights the police patrol the streets and any person with something missing has to go to the police station."

Comment on the roads was frank, "Many of the new roads run helter skelter for they have not been planed or proply constructed", and, "There are very few corners free from objects obstructing the view in all directions", which must have been particularly dangerous since, "There are street lights in some places but they don't work."

And what could be more terse and to the point than, "The sides of the road are shocking."

Although candid in their criticisms the children were not averse to offering possible remedies, "First, I would see that all roads had curved corners."

And lest the city fathers should object to the expense it was recommended that, "Drunken drivers should be fined. The increase thus obtained in the Town's Treasury could be put to increasing the amount of macadam", which, while perhaps being a reflection on the sobriety of the citizens was at least a practical suggestion.

Sotto voce.
Drunken voice.

However, drunks are not the only problem. One observant youngster had noticed a car, "driven by a nervous newly licensed lady".

Another child, doubtless feeling the authorities were not sufficiently aware of the traffic problems in their own town was prepared to go to extreme lengths to bring them to their attention, "All aldermen should walk, or ride a bicycle for a week."

As might be expected, the police did not escape attention and one bright youth suggested, "Give a reward for every conviction a policeman makes. This will make them keener on their job."

But one little girl, conscious of her own limitations, washed her hands of the whole problem, "As I don't know much about cars, I can't do much to improve Road Safety for them."

A surefooted animal is an animal that when
it kicks it does not miss.

4. Child art

One of the nicest things about children's work is its forth-rightness and honesty. Even the more imaginative efforts reveal this, for example, "Once upon a time, a poor woman lived in England. William was her son. One day his mother said i have no money in the house. William was very sad. He could not get what he wanted now.

So they lived unhappily ever after."

That was written by an eight-year-old. At that age a child's creative efforts are controlled by what he knows, rather than by what he sees or can imagine. So, if the following remarks on why a boy should learn to cook appear to be amusing, they are not meant to be so but are presented as irrefutable facts, "Boys should learn to cook because if their mothers are sick, they can make the dinner."

"When men join the army there are usually no ladies with them, so that men must cook the food."

To a child there are no such things as anachronisms. 'Once upon a time' is now, and so, when a class of nine-year-olds was asked after a Scripture lesson to make a picture of the Flight into Egypt, a number of children drew Mary pushing Jesus in a pram, and one boy made a picture of an aeroplane with four passengers, three of them wearing halos.

The aeroplane was explained by the use of the word 'Flight' and the three passengers with halos were ob-

Dieu et mon droit!
My God, and you're right.

viously meant to represent Joseph, Mary and the Holy Child. But the fourth figure remained a mystery until the young artist revealed that it was 'Ponshus the pilot'.

Art lessons can be revealing. The child mind is direct and free from the conventions and inhibitions that plague the adult. There are few subjects he is unwilling to tackle although an occasional one does crop up.

A teacher having prepared the class by describing such picturesque people as butchers, waitresses, soldiers, sailors and other uniformed wage-earners asked them to make a picture of what they wanted to be when they grew up.

They set to with a will depicting themselves as nurses, members of the armed forces, postmen, railway engineers and pop stars. But one little girl sat with a puzzled expression on her face and a blank sheet of paper in front of her.

'What's the matter, Jane?' asked the teacher.
'I can't draw my picture,' said Jane.
'Why dear, what is it you want to be?'
'I want to be married,' Jane replied bluntly.

Jane was an unusual girl. Not because she wanted to be married, but because she couldn't find a symbol for marriage.

Below the age of eight or nine, child art is made up from symbols. These are perfectly adequate and can rarely be mistaken for anything but what they represent.

A group of children was asked to make a picture of a famous person and the teacher, as teachers do, wandered about looking at their efforts.

Most high roads were bridal paths in the
eighteenth century.

'And who are you painting, dear?' she asked
one child.

'I'm painting God.'

'But nobody knows what God looks like,' said
the teacher.

'They will when I've finished,' replied the child
without even bothering to look up.

An understanding of child art depends on an understanding of the symbols they use, but sometimes even that
is not enough and it is necessary to seek an explanation
from the artist himself.

A class was told the story of St George, which is about
a beautiful princess who was chained to a rock so that a
fierce dragon could devour her. She was saved at the last
minute by the fortuitous arrival of the handsome knight
on his white charger.

When the story was ended the teacher asked the children to make a picture. Only a few minutes elapsed when
a little boy came out and said, 'I've finished.' And he
showed her his picture. There was the usual blue strip at
the top to symbolise the sky and a green strip at the
bottom which represented the ground. And in the middle
there was a brown triangle which obviously stood for the
rocks where the story took place. The stage was set, but
the actors were missing – or were they?

'Yes, that's very nice, dear,' said the teacher.
'But where is the beautiful princess?'

'She's round the other side of the rocks,' replied
Wilbur.

'And the dragon, where's the horrible dragon?'

'The dragon's in the cave. It's dark in the cave.

The Knight saved the maiden from
a horrible dragoon.

You can't see the dragon.'
'Oh, but where is St George and his lovely white
horse?'
'Well, he hasn't come yet.'

And Wilbur, seven years old, picked up his picture and
returned to his seat with the air of having satisfactorily
completed an interesting but not too difficult task.

Coup de grâce.
A lawn mower.

5. 'Dear Sir, or madman'

Not all howlers are perpetrated in the classroom. Quite a number of them come in letters written by youngsters separated from their parents by boarding school or holiday camp. Many a fond mother has been the recipient of at least one letter that has contained a phrase that made her smile, or perhaps unfortunately, made her gasp with alarm. What emotions must have been stirred when the postman delivered the following, "Dere Mum, something exciting happened today your loving son Pete X X X"

No child can ever understand how even the most casual reference to his personal welfare is seized on by his mother to be read and worried over as she searches for that elusive something she suspects is 'hidden between the lines'. And it is understandable that she should keep the refrigerator well stocked following her little boy's protracted absence from home when she gets a letter which states bluntly, "I wish I was at home where I could get some sensible food, not just starch. How do they expect me to do well at track and swimming on starch?"

The youngster who wrote from camp, "I forgot to tell you that a person is not allowed to put stuff on his hair. My counsellor says it isn't manly. I've got dandruff", never knew what a nasty blow he had delivered.

Not surprisingly, sport often features in letters home, together with uninhibited criticism of fellow performers.

Charon was the man who fried soles
over the sticks.

"We had the relays and we came second. Last year we were first. The trouble is the new kids. They're terrible, not one runner amongst them. All they've got is brains. They're useless."

And the following must have raised a smile when mother read,

"Many new faces toed the line at the track meet."

But as time goes on, the tone of the letters changes and other interests apart from food and sport become apparent.

Mother begins to realise her little boy is growing up.

"The under-sixteen swimming team, of which I am a distinguished member, won and we got a trophy. The first trophy the school has won for swimming for a very long time. There was a girl diving. She wasn't so pretty but boy, could she dive. And her figure was perfect (sorry I'm being such a wolf, dad, but you know how it is)."

But, *mens sana in corpore sano*, the healthy body gives rise to comments from the healthy mind and mention of learning and culture occur from time to time, "I went to a concert last night. There was a fellow playing a fiddle and a lady on a piano. The violinist was a Pole. The music was classical and I fell asleep. So did a lot of other chaps."

Interest in the arts does not stop with music. Sooner or later, the Old Folks at home are entertained by their son's profound comments on drama, "We went to see the second part of Henry IV played at the University. I thought it was quite good and there were a lot of girls there as well."

A polygon is a man with two wives.

While letters from children to their parents are often funny, sometimes revealing and nearly always entertaining, they are as nothing compared to the letters parents write to the teachers about their children. Often there is a delightful ambiguity about examples such as the following which keeps a harrassed teacher happy for days.

"Please sir, Billy's ill with swellings in his throat and the doctor says it's a gathering of the clans."

"Please sir, Excuse Freddy's absence from school. I had a baby. It wasn't his fault."

Sometimes the note has to be written by the child himself in which case anything can happen.

"Dere sir, I can't get to school. Mother is in bed with ten disciples."

Perhaps only this teacher would understand that *ten disciples* was really appendicitis.

Of the absentees for whom excuses have to be made, large numbers seem to suffer from disorders of a kind that would baffle a whole College of Physicians. How, for instance, would they prescribe for Rickie whose mother asked teacher to excuse his being away from school because, "his face is all coming out through his stomach".

Or for Randy who, "had a stomach ache since Saturday through a bottle of pop and it hasn't gone off yet".

But we feel that the teacher who received the following might have been justified in suspecting its apparent ambiguity.

"Dere sir, Kindly excuse Jimmy's absence from school yesterday. He fell in the river. By doing same, you will oblige."

Militia non est jocus.
It is no joke to be in the army.

6. Do-it-yourself English

Among children to whom English is a foreign language, confusion is worse confounded when they have to deal with their teacher's spoken word. Even among those to whom it is their mother tongue, the word they hear often means something quite different from the same word if they could see it. Here is a list of popular words heard but not understood.

Acoustic: A thing used in billiards for hitting the ball.

Auto: As in: I auto go out.

Axe: A query as in: I axe you this question.

Balks: A container as in: Put it in the balks.

Coincide: A direction as in: Coincide it is cold out here.

Dare: A place as in: Put it in dare.

Debate: Something used in fishing, I put debate on the hook.

Did: Passed away as in: He was did when we got there.

Gladiator: What the cannibal said.

Gull: Female as in: She's my gull friend.

Oily: Time, the opposite of late as in: It's too oily to go home yet.

Sore: Viewed as in: I sore it on tv.

Use: Personal pronoun as in: Use guys going fishing?

Violin: A bad hotel.

Hors de combat.
A war horse.

Place howlers

Brussels is famous for sprouts and carpets.

The British Isles has a temporary climate.

The population of California is getting a bit too thick.

The inhabitants of Moscow are called mosquitoes.

The inhabitants of Paris are called Parisites.

Only on the back of buses do they have smoking aloud.

In France even the phesants drink wine.

Tarzan is a short name for the American flag. Its full name is Tarzan Stripes.

Sienna is a place in Italy famous for being burnt.

Q. Name six animals to be found in the Arctic.
A. Three bears and three seals.

Another name for Gaul is vinegar.

There is a great deal of nothing in the middle of Australia.

The Philistines are islands near Japan.

The Pope lives in a Vacuum.

A synagogue is a place where sinners worship like a church only Jewish.

In Vancouver you can tell it's summer because the rain gets warmer.

Stirling is in Scotland and it is noted for silver.

Famous people use a different name when they travel in the Congo.

The cistern chapel is where Mickel Angelo painted the selling.

The Sewage Canal is in Egypt.

Biblical howlers

Jacob had a brother called Seesaw.

Noah's wife was Joan of Arc.

Sunday school teacher: Does anyone remember who Peter was?

Child: I think he was a wabbit.

'And some fell on stony ground and the fowls of the air sprang up and choked them.'

An epistle is the wife of an apostle.

Palsy is what a man in the Bible was sick of. It's a sort of new writer's dance.

The Israelites made a golden calf because they didn't have enough gold for a cow.

'Remember that thou keep holy the Sabbath Day. Six days shalt thou labour and do no work.'

Solomon had 300 wives and a lot of cucumbers.

The first commandment was when Eve told Adam to eat the apple.

'... there was manna in the dessert ...'

A republican is a sinner in the Bible.

Acrimony is what they call marriage in the Bible so it is sometimes holy.

Abraham is in the Bible and is noted for his bosom.

Solomon had three hundred porcupines.

Alias was a man in the Bible.

Q. Who said: 'God's in His heaven, all's right with the world'?

A. Mrs God.

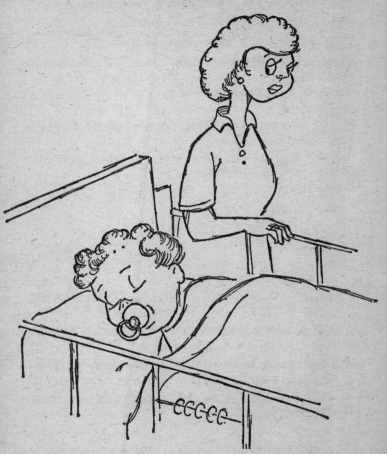

A Job's comforter is what you give to babies
to keep them quiet.

Right Royal howlers

The King wore a scarlet robe trimmed with vermin.

The feminine of drake is Queen Elizabeth.

Chinese kings used to be called mandolines.

Queen Elizabeth was called the Virgil Queen because she knew Latin.

William the Conqueror brought the Mormons to England.

Henry VIII was a good king. He liked plenty of money, plenty of wives and died of ulcers on his leg.

King Arthur had some brave soldiers. He called them the Knuts of the Round Table.

Henry VIII had an abess on his knee and he quarelled with the Pope.

The King and Queen sat on two thorns.

In Valasquez's portrait of Philip IV, the moustache is well placed. It is an excellent portrait because it gives the wrong impression of Philip.

Henry VIII had the Prayer Book put into English to spite the Pope who wanted to marry Catherine of Arragon.

Henry VIII had a sore leg as well as being a Nonconformist.

England used to be Roman Catholic then Elizabeth made it Christian.

The King was not allowed to order taxis without the consent of Parliament.

My favourite character in History is Henry VIII
because he had eight wives and killed them all.

Occupational howlers

Joan of Arc's father was a poor pheasant.

A hostage is a nice lady on an aeroplane.

A glazier is a man who slides down mountains in places like Alaska.

A buttress is a female butcher.

The lady next door is a famous church-woman. She washes the Sunday school teas.

An optimist is a man who looks after your eyes and a pessimist is a man who looks after your feet.

In the old morality boys played girls' parts so they were not as moral as you might think.

The footballers certainly worked as a team, weaving and unweaving their combinations.

The Minister of War is sometimes called a pardray by the soldiers.

A bank manager leads a sedimentary life.

A deacon is a thing you pile on the top of a hill and set fire to it to warn the people the enemy is coming. A priest is a man in the Old Testament. I never seen a bishop so I don't know what it is.

An optimist looks on the best side and a pianist looks on the worst side.

Fidel Castro invented Castro oil.

Our Minister comes sometimes to take the Bible class. At other times a gentleman takes it.

Q. What are rabies? What would you do for them?
A. Rabies are Jewish priests. I would do nothing for them.

Aristocrats are men who do tricks on the stage.

A pessimist is a man who is never happy unless he is miserable. Even then, he is not pleased.

A parsimonious person is a man who wants to be a parson.

Degas was extremely fond of painting ballet dancers and other objects.

In some games of golf you have to play with a handy cup.

Vergil was a man who worked in a church.

Plato was the god of the Underground.

Mr Wilson has been in labour ever since he entered politics.

A bibulous man is a preacher or a Sunday school teacher.

A knave is a man who digs holes to put pipes in.

Zero was a Roman king who played the fiddle.

Musical howlers

Waltz time is sometimes called cripple time.

D. C. in music stands for, 'Don't Clap'.

Ruby Tanyer is a song about waves.

Ladies who sing a low kind of songs are called con-traltos.

A trombone is an instrument you play by pulling it in and out.

An oboe is sometimes called a bum.

The smallest wind instrument is the piccadilly.

Human Biology howlers

Phlebitis is a disease which you can get if you don't wash your dog.

A skeleton is someone with his outside off.

Blood consists of red corkscrews and white corkscrews.

The heart is a comical mussel which is divided into four parts by a petition.

Lumbago is a mineral. They make pencils from it.

Breathing is made up of two things, first inspiration, second expectoration.

Germs are sort of small insecks that get in you if you touch somebody that's got some. Some are called mumps and measles and hooping coff.

Etiquette is the noise you make when you sneeze.

The heart is a big working mussel. It is full of bright red blood and all over the rest of the body we have only dirty blood.

My brother comes out in spots because of his allegory.

A phlegmatic person coughs a lot and clears his throat.

The home of the swallow is in the stomick.

Women's sufferage is what they have suffer at child birth.

Lovers call the heart the seat of love but doctors know it aint.

Psychology is a fairly modern disease discovered by a man called Floyd.

You can easy tell a drunkard's heart it is fat all over, but a good heart is all nice and clean.

When a person is susceptible to something they are called septic. Boys in love often are.

Leges utiles hominibus sunt.
Legs are useful to men.

Mathematical howlers

To bisex angels you need a protector.

A triangle with all its sides equal is called an equatorial.

LXX stands for love and kisses.

Parallel lines can't meet unless you bend them.

An oxygen has eight sides.

In a right angle triangle the square on the hippopotamus is equal.

A quotation is the answer to a division sum.

Two straight lines cannot enclose a space unless they are bent.

A circle is a round line equal from the middle which you can't see where it begins.

Gross darkness is one hundred and forty-four times as dark as ordinary dark.

An octet is in geometry. It has eight sides.
Parallel lines are lines which get nearer together as they get further apart.

Philosophy increases thirty-two feet per second.

A line is a length with no breath.

A curve is the longest way between two points.

A trapezium is what they swing on in a sircus.

Gender howlers

Gender is the destruction of sex.

A fort is a place to put men soldiers in and a fortress is a place to put women soldiers in.

The masculine of lass is ass.

The masculine of ladybird sounds as if it should be gentlemanbird, but that looks funny.

The masculine of vixen is vicar.

The feminine of manager is menagerie.

The Gorgons had long snakes in their hair. They looked like women only more horrible.

Celibacy was the name of a very wise man.

The masculine of dam is dash.

The wife of Columbus was Columbine.

A widow is a wife without a man.

In the old days a woman soldier was called Amazing.

The wife of a duke is a ducky.

'Ster' is a female suffix. Example, spinster, monster and sterile.

Manpower is the extra strength man has more than a woman.

The masculine of Duchess is Duck.

Geographical howlers

Q. If you stand facing the north, what do you have on your left hand?
A. Fingers.

An average is something it rains on.

A watershed is where water is stored something like a barn.

Volcanoes spew saliva.

There are a lot of currants in the sea.

The Eskimos are God's frozen people.

Imports are ports that are far inland.

Hot currants keep the port free of ice in winter.

A consonant is a large piece of land. There are five consonants, Europe, Africa and America and two others.

A compass tells a man where he ought to go and it always points up the Pole.

The tropical air was soft and putrid.

The temperate zone is a place where nobody drinks too much.

The horizon is a line where the sea and the sky meet but isn't there when you get there.

Some of the bellowing sheiks is very rich because of all that oil.

An Equinox is a native of Iceland.

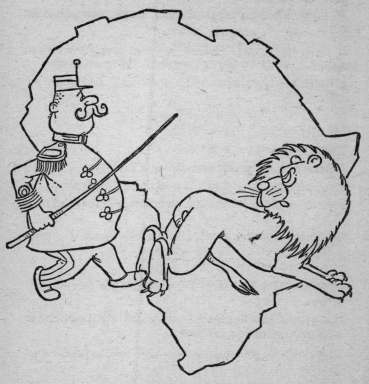

**The Equator is a menagerie lion running round
the earth through Africa.**

Natural History howlers

The dodo is a bird that is now decent. There are a lot of other decent things.

To kill a butterfly, moth or other inseck, you pinch its borax.

A cuckoo is a bird what lays other birds' eggs in its nest.

A hostage has long legs, a long neck and nice feathers.

A magnet is something to be found in a bad apple or other fruit.

The opposite of evergreen is nevergreen.

There are eligible fish in the sea.

Pineapples grow on pine trees.

When a dog has puppies it's called a litre.

Some cows are very dangerous especially the bull.

In sandstorms, the camels put their heads in the sand and let it find its own destination.

Terra cotta is stuff squeezed out of a little inseck and used to turn cakes and puddings and things red.

A blizzard is the inside of a chicken.

Scales are what fish have. They are like fur on cats and feathers on hens.

Oyster feathers come from South Africa. They used to be in fashion but they're not now.

A convoy is a collection of some birds like cartridges.

Moths eat hardly nothing only holes.

Herrings go about the sea in shawls.

Kangaroos are poached animals.

The main feeders of the Amazon and Orinoco
are alligators.

A prism is a kind of dried plum because people say 'prunes and prisms' when they have a photygraph taken.

The apostle is the only pouched animal in America.

A ruminating animal chews its cubs.

Mushrooms look like umbrellas because they grow where it's wet.

Q. What animal do you associate with Lady Godiva?
A. Bear.

Cattle and pigs are bought on the stock market.

A Papal bull is a male cow.

Tadpoles eat one another till they become frogs.

Marsupials are poached animals.

A centimetre is an insect with a hundred legs.

People go to Africa to hunt rhinostriches.

Grammatical howlers

A relative pronoun is a family pronoun such as, father, sister, cousin!

The future of 'I give' is 'you take'.

The bowels are: a, e, i, o, u and sometimes w and y.

Q. Write a sentence containing the word 'summit'.
A. There is summit the matter.

The possessive case is when somebody has got yours and won't give it up.

Q. Is 'trousers' singular or plural?
A. It's singular at the top and plural at the bottom.

Letters in thin sloping type are in hysterics.

'His face was covered with black bread ...'

The plural of forget-me-not is forget-us-nots.

The plural of spouse is spice.

'Near the corpse stood the old barn.'

He was persecuted for taking brides.

The word 'fetish' means when people are merry like going to a fete.

An abstract noun is the name of something that does not exist like goodness.

The degrees of bad are: bad, very sick, dead.

To know where to put the verb, subject, object, etc. is something for a boy to be proud of.

Poetry is when every line starts with a capital letter.

A simile is a picturesque way of saying what you really mean, such as saying your father is a square.

'The lady smiled at him displacing a beautiful set of white teeth.'

A monologue is a dialogue for one person.

'What angle wakes me from my floury bed?'

A passive verb is when the subject is the sufferer, as 'I am loved'.

'But' is a conjunction because it shows a sort of connection like between a goat and a man.

A metaphor is a suppressed smile.

They went to rescue the damsel in distress and they were sexful.

Q. Write a sentence beginning with 'than'.
A. 'Than' is a word of four letters.

The lady broke a bottle of champain across the bows then to the delight of the crowd she slipped slowly and majestically down the greasy slipway into the sea.

My father is in the Middle Ages.

Little boy showing Granny his dog, 'Granny, say hello to your grandog.'

From a thank you letter after schoolchildren had visited a lumber yard: 'Thank you for letting us see your lovely broads.'

The people were ground down by heavy taxis.

Infra dig means in lodgings.

Only respectable people are illegible to get credit.

The word sepulchre from 'se' negative and 'pulchre' fair. So it means an ugly place.

A sleeping partner is a man who goes to sleep playing bridge.

Scientific howlers

Water is composed of Oxygin and Hydrogin. Oxygin is pure but Hydrogin is gin and water.

Chlorine gas is very dangerous to humans so it should be an experiment only performed on the teacher.

Heat moves through water with conviction.

The thermoneter is an instrument for measuring temperance.

Atomic weights are used for weighing atoms.

To fill a flask with acidulated water, turn on the tap and acidulate.

When you look in a mirror, the angel of reflection is the same as the angel of incidents.

Water boils at a higher temperature in a Fahrenheit thermometer than it does in a Celsius.

Ammonium chloride is sometimes called silly maniac.

Skyscrapers are a kind of telescope.

If you squeeze the juice out of mud you get dust.

An emolument is a sort of medicine.

There are four elements, mustard, salt, pepper and vinegar although I think vinegar is reely an acid.

A good cosmetic is salt and water. Cosmetics make you sick.

Gravity is that which if there was none,
we should all fly away.

Literary howlers

Bacon was the man who wrote Shakespeare.

Poetry is a thing you make prose of.

Shakespeare wrote tragedies, comedies and errors.

Handel was a little boy in a tale with his sister called Handel and Grettel.

Polonius was a sort of sausage.

Homer wrote the Oddity.

Esau was a slave who wrote fables and sold his copyright for a mess of potash.

Tom Sawyer was a smart boy. His character was always good sometimes.

There are some passages in Shakespeare which are quite pretty, such as 'spoil the rod and bare the child', and lots of others.

No one has yet succeeded in edifying the Dark Lady of the Sonnets.

Scheherazade was Bluebeard's wife for a thousand nights, so no wonder she was able to tell so many tales.

'I took thee for thy better.' This is what Hamlet said when he stabbed Polonius and thought he was a rat.

The appendix is a part of the book for which nobody has found much use.

Napoleon was sent to Melba.

Shakespeare lived at Windsor with his Merry Wives.

I can't remember his name but he was the poet who wrote about the first fine careless rupture.

Shakespeare wrote a book called lamb's tails.

The Pied Piper told the mayor he could get rid of all the rates.

I think it was Touchstone who said, 'Where is fancy bread?'

'The child is father to the man.' This was written by Shakespeare. He didn't often make that kind of mistake.

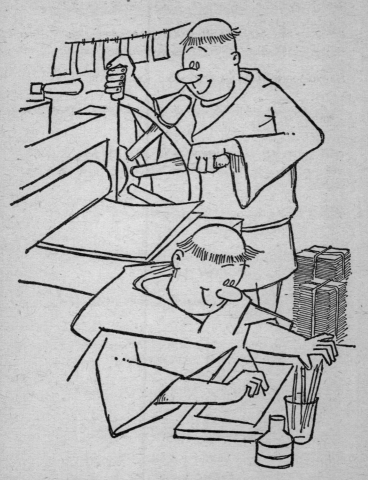

A monastery is a place where they make money.

Historical howlers

Geneva had long hair. She rode a white horse and nobody had to look.

Wolsey saved his life by dying before he got to London.

Clive committed suicide three times.

The Ancient Britons used to fish in cockles. There are still some cockles in Wales.

The Black Hole of Calcutta was when 146 men were shut in a room with one small widow. Only three came out alive.

Q. Write a brief essay on Carpaccio.
A. Very little is known about Carpaccio.

Marshal Goering was a fat man because he was one of Hitler's stoutest supporters.

The Invisible Armada had to wait while Drake finished his game of bowels.

Washington was a great general who always began a battle with the fixed determination to win or lose.

During the Napoleonic Wars crowned heads were trembling in their shoes.

Socrates died from an overdose of wedlock.

Sir Walter Raleigh brought tobacco from America. He called it tobacco after the Greek god Baccus who taught people how to get drunk.

The Normans put mokes round their castles.

Before the French Revolution men at the slightest suggestion of scorn or ridicule, challenged that person to a duel. So they lived a life of pleasure.

In Memlings time all pictures were painted individually as of course photography was unknown.

Fate gave Reynolds good manners and Fortune gave him sufficient means to enjoy them.

Hitler wanted to invade England and he got a lot of flat-bottomed bargees.

Pas de deux.
Father of twins.

Miscellaneous Definitions

Dusk is little bits fluff you find under the bed.

A lie is an abomination unto the Lord but a very present help in time of trouble.

Barbarians are little balls they put in bicycles to make the wheels run smooth.

Reefs are what you put on coffins.

Necessity is the mother of convention.

Insects is burned in some churches.

A graven image is a nice grave stone.

A Poll Tax is paid by everybody who has a head.

The Navy is sometimes called the senile service.

Chaplets are little churches.

A Trade Union is a place you go when you get fired.

Austerity is an old religion but today even politicians preach it.

The modern era is the mistakes being made today.

Catholics have to believe what the Pope tells them but Protestants can believe what they like.

The stoics didn't believe in nothing much. You could hurt them and they didn't cry.

Saturnine means gloomy-looking. Saturn was the god of agriculture.

A fan is a thing to blow the warm air off with.

An idolator is a very idle person.

Genius is an infinite capacity for picking brains.

Brutes are imperfect animals. Man alone is a perfect beast.

Income is a yearly tax.

Petroleum is what you cover floors with if you don't use parky.

Parsimony is the money that is left after ma gets the housekeeping.

A surname is the name of somebody you say 'Sir' to.

A cyclone is a sort of bicycle they ride in a sircus. It's only got one wheel.

Faith is believing what you know is untrue.

A telephone is a funny thing you can talk into from a long way off with something at the other end for the person to hear with that you listen to.

An anachronism is a thing that was in the past before it has taken place in the future.

Q. What is a cyclone?
A. God made them. It sucks.

Ambiguity is telling the truth when you don't mean to.

An epitaph is a short sarcastic poem.

**A refugee is a man who takes charge at
a football match.**

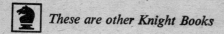 *These are other Knight Books*

Richard Gregory

KNIGHT MINE OF USELESS INFORMATION

Did you know that 100 million bottles of Coca-Cola are drunk each day? Or that crocodiles have a semi-transparent third eyelid which slides over the eye when they are submerged? Or that if all the corks of all the wine bottles produced in France each year were glued together, they would encircle the earth ten times? Fascinate your friends with these and other items of useless information!

KNIGHT BOOK OF RIDDLES

Do you know why good bread is like the sun? Or what is hot when it's cold? Or when a cat is really a sailing boat? This book will tell you. Hundreds of riddles about birds, animals, people, cities; riddles from 'My sister Kate' and riddles in rhyme.

Falcon Travis

KNIGHT BOOK OF PASS-TIME GAMES

Have you ever been on a long journey by car, train or coach with nothing to do? Waited on a platform, in a traffic jam or a lay-by? Here are lots of simple games to while away the time for one player or more. Most require nothing, others just a pencil and paper.

KNIGHT BOOK OF SECRET CODES

Enjoy exchanging secret messages with your friends which no one else will understand!
You can learn all about poly-alpha ciphers, code grilles, symbols, acrostics, invisible inks and special code words like owl and hawk. And there's one section on codes and ciphers in games and contests, and another on how to be a code-breaker.
Everything you need to be a super sleuth!

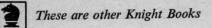 *These are other Knight Books*

Ann and John Robson

WORD GAMES FOR ALL THE FAMILY

These can be played at any time – even at mealtimes
and on long journeys. They need no equipment – not
even pencil and paper. They can be played by anyone,
from Mum and Dad to the youngest just beginning to
speak. Mind-stretching, ingenious, fun!

Ask your local bookseller, or at your public library, for
details of other Knight Books, or write to the Editor-
in-Chief, Knight Books, Arlen House, Salisbury Road,
Leicester LE1 7QS